You're Going to Be My Mom!

You're Going to Be My Mom!

A 40-WEEK DEVOTIONAL JOURNEY THROUGH YOUR PREGNANCY

Astrid Rivera, M.D., L.C.C.E.

CHRISTIAN PUBLICATIONS, INC.

CAMP HILL, PENNSYLVANIA

✠ CHRISTIAN PUBLICATIONS, INC.

3825 Hartzdale Drive, Camp Hill, PA 17011
www.christianpublications.com

Faithful, biblical publishing since 1883

You're Going to Be My Mom!
ISBN: 0-88965-229-5
LOC Control Number: 2004114367
© 2005 by Astrid Rivera
All rights reserved
Printed in Korea

05 06 07 08 09 5 4 3 2 1

Preface

Congratulations! You're going to be a mom! Pregnancy is a wonderful unity of physical, emotional and spiritual experiences. The prenatal meditations included in *You're Going to Be My Mom!* have been written with the purpose of uncovering this tri-dimensional view of motherhood.

You're Going to Be My Mom! will take you on a forty-week journey through the various developmental stages of the growing fetus. The meditations are narrated by the yet-to-be-born baby who will share some spiritual insights about the significance of pregnancy and parenthood. Each meditation will be followed by a brief prayer of response for you, Mom. Feel free to add your own thoughts and feelings to this prayer.

Additionally, the weekly devotionals will include a section called "Growth Guide" that will track the progression of physical changes occurring inside your body during your forty-week journey.

Human life is as precious as it is fragile. It is impossible to sustain life's full magnitude in one's strength alone; therefore, the very Author of the miracle of life has prepared everything you need to achieve it together.

A mother and her unborn child are the most vulnerable of all creatures. The baby must rely on his/her mother to be formed and birthed. The mother, in turn, must depend on the support and love of her husband in order to carry out her sublime assignment. Unfortunately, in many homes today the father may not be present to help with the raising of the child. In these cases, other friends and family members, along with the support of a local church, will give the expectant mother the strength and encouragement she will need.

These nine months are the most precious time to become attuned to your own body, your baby and your Creator. On these pages you will find scientific knowledge interwoven with biblical truths to help you discover the compelling beauty of being a woman and being "born" as a mother along with your child.

Being a mother is an attribute of the creative love of God the Father, the saving love of the Son and the forming love of the Holy Spirit inside you.

Welcome to the wonderful world of motherhood!

Astrid Rivera, M.D., L.C.C.E
Kennesaw, Georgia

Before Time...

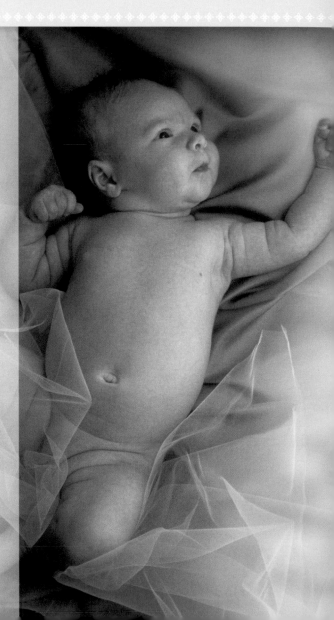

I knew you

before I formed

you in your

mother's

womb.

Jeremiah 1:5

$\mathscr{M}$om, did you know that
I existed in the mind of our
Creator God even before the
beginning of all time? He has a
perfect knowledge of us. I know
that's really hard to imagine,
but what a powerful and loving
heavenly Father He must be!
Just think—in His big master
plan God chose *you* to nurture
me until I'm ready to make my
grand entrance into the world! I
can't wait to see your face and
cuddle up in your loving arms.

Mom's Response:

Dear God, You are the mighty
Creator of all things. Your deeds are
beyond my comprehension. Your
personal care for Your children is
worthy of all my praise. You are
from everlasting to everlasting, the
great I AM. Thank You for this
wonderful gift You are about to give
me. Amen.

Cells have forty-six
chromosomes, forty-four
of which provide physical
characteristics and the
remaining two provide sexual
inheritance: XX for female and
XY for male. The sexual cells
contain only one-half of the
genetic material of a normal
cell, and this makes them
targets for the immune system.

Normally, one egg matures
each month and lives only
twenty-four hours. While it
waits on the outer third of the
fallopian tube for the sperm cell
to arrive, nurse cells surround
it, feeding and protecting
it. The nurse cells also hide
the egg from the unrelenting
immunological cells, always
hunting for atypical cells.

[NOTE: You can find
additional information about
the highlighted words in the
glossary at the end of this book.]

Day One...

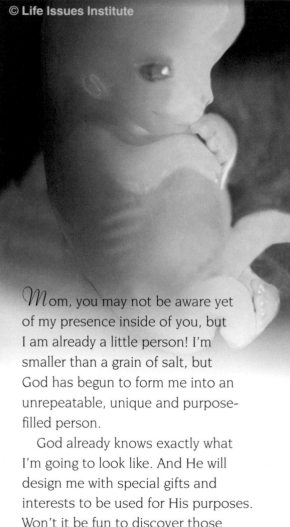

You saw me before I was born. Every day of my life was recorded in your book.

Psalm 139:16

Mom, you may not be aware yet of my presence inside of you, but I am already a little person! I'm smaller than a grain of salt, but God has begun to form me into an unrepeatable, unique and purpose-filled person.

God already knows exactly what I'm going to look like. And He will design me with special gifts and interests to be used for His purposes. Won't it be fun to discover those unique traits together?

10

Mom's Response:

Gracious heavenly Father,
how I praise You and
thank You for this precious
new life that You are
forming inside my body.
Take hold of my hand,
Lord, as we walk through
this unchartered journey
together. And please help
our family fulfill Your plan
for our lives. Amen.

GROWTH GUIDE

While the egg waits, the sperm cells swim vigorously upstream, overcoming one obstacle after another by using wisely all the available resources. Sperm cells swim in large teams thanks to energy supplied by the seminal fluid and enzymes present in the prostatic fluid. The seminal fluid is alkaline in order to neutralize the lethal acidity of the vagina. Thanks to this protection, many sperm cells are able to cross the labyrinth of the cervical mucous. The mucous plug is normally impenetrable, but it softens for a brief twenty-four hours every month with the only purpose of allowing fertilization by the sperm cells.

It has been an extraordinary selection process: Only 1 among 350 million sperm cells and 1 among 120,000 eggs have joined to become a unique and unrepeatable creature. After fertilization, the new human being is called a zygote and has adopted the egg as his/her first home.

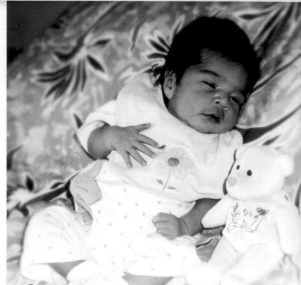

> *Thank you for making me so wonderfully complex! Your workmanship is marvelous.*
>
> *Psalm 139:14*

*M*om, it will take me about a week to make the delicate journey to my new home inside of you. And even though I'm only a little speck, a lot of amazing changes are going on inside of me during this trip: My hair and eye color have been determined, my future height has been established and the biggest question— whether I'll be a boy or a girl—has already been decided!

To think that our heavenly Father—the Creator of the whole universe—would care about all these tiny details in my life is truly breathtaking.

Mom's Response:

Dear Lord, You are an awesome God, but I have to admit that I'm a little overwhelmed with the thought of bringing a brand new human being into this world. Please be my daily Strength and Guide. I need Your help. Amen.

GROWTH GUIDE

The fertilized egg starts its trip toward the **uterus**, gently pushed by the **cilia** inside the fallopian tube. It is a long journey—four to five inches (ten to twelve centimeters) long. Its internal diameter is still the same as the original egg.

By the end of the journey, the new human being has undergone seven divisions, forming a perfect sixty-four-cell **morula**. Meanwhile, in the **ovary**, the **yellow body** (*corpus luteum*) carries out the very important role of producing the **hormone progesterone**. The yellow body is the vestige of the **follicle** where the egg was liberated, and it releases the hormone in order to sustain pregnancy until the **placenta** takes over this vital function.

Week Two...

> *You . . . knit*
>
> *me together in*
>
> *my mother's*
>
> *womb.*
>
> Psalm 139:13

$\mathcal{M}$om, this week I finally finished my long journey. And now that I've made it to my new location, you are considered to be officially "pregnant with child." Congratulations! Incredibly, God has built into me everything I will need to survive and thrive here for the next thirty-nine weeks. My new home is splendid, warm and tender. It is in this environment where God will shape me physically, emotionally and spiritually.

I love you, Mommy—you are my universe.

Mom's Response:

Heavenly Father, up until now my world has pretty much revolved around ME. But now I see that I have a much greater role to play in the life of my child. Teach me, Lord, how to love others more than myself. Amen.

GROWTH GUIDE

The **endometrium** is a dynamic tissue covering the walls of the uterus and is fully renewed every month. The endometrium, rich in blood vessels and glands, is splendidly prepared for the arrival of the baby, now called a **blastocyst.** The arrival of the blastocyst to the interior of the uterus is urgent because its capacity to expand outward has reached the limit. From now on, inside the mother's **womb,** the blastocyst will begin to expand its territory while it continues its accelerated multiplication.

By the end of this week, the **implantation** process will be finished. The contact areas between the bodies of the mother and the baby "hug" each other and begin to interweave microscopically by means of finger-like cellular projections. This is the future site of the placenta.

Twenty-five percent of pregnancies do not reach this stage because abnormal blastocysts are spontaneously expulsed with the next **menstruation.** These **miscarriages** are unnoticed by most women.

Week Three...

> *You made all
> the delicate,
> inner parts of
> my body.*
>
> Psalm 139:13

$\mathcal{M}$om, by the time you start to miss your period, I am already firmly installed in my new home! There is a lot of activity inside me with things moving in all directions. Cellular networks are stretching, bending or specializing. And I can imagine there must be a lot of conflicting feelings inside you as well! Pretty soon, both of our hearts will begin to beat together!

I wish you could see how I am developing *each moment of every hour*. God is at work even while both of us are sleeping!

My **umbilical cord** will keep me attached to you through the placenta, which has the ability to filter out a lot of harmful substances. But things like alcohol, drugs and tobacco can pass through it. So please take care of yourself, Mommy, because I am now completely dependent on you.

Mom's Response:

*Loving Father, give me Your wisdom
to make the right choices about my
body. I want to provide the safest
environment possible for my little
one. Amen.*

GROWTH GUIDE

At this point the level of the hormone known as **HCG** can be detected by early lab tests. As the baby is nested firmly, the rudimentary placenta has started to work, releasing the hormones required to support the pregnancy. The whole chorionic sac measures less than one centimeter in diameter. The **(EDD) estimated delivery date** is calculated by adding forty weeks from the first day of your last period. In practice, the end of pregnancy is determined by the maturity of the baby's lungs and could be between weeks thirty-eight and forty-two of pregnancy.

As the implantation process takes place, the blastocyst starts to develop the amnios, chorion and embryonic disc, which will form not only all the structures of the new human being, but the amniotic fluid, the amniotic sac, placenta and umbilical cord as well. Everything developed out of the same original cell!

Week Four…

> *O LORD, you*
>
> *have examined*
>
> *my heart*
>
> *and know*
>
> *everything*
>
> *about me.*
>
> *Psalm 139:1*

$\mathcal{M}$om, by the time your pregnancy test shows positive, my heart has already been beating for a little while. Thank you for choosing to preserve my life and to bring me into your loving family. Our heavenly Father is very pleased with you, Mommy, because you have chosen to obey His words to "multiply and fill the earth"!

This week all my organs began to form. The first one to fully function is my heart. It beats approximately 140 times a minute (twice as fast as yours). When I'm scared, the rate increases just like yours! My life will be preserved in the sanctuary of your body until the moment I am ready to come out to meet you.

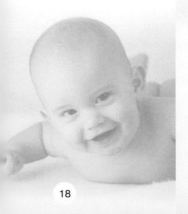

Mom's Response:

Dear Lord, it's so hard to believe that another life is growing inside of me. Thank You, Father God, for making me a woman and for the beautiful miracle of reproduction!
Amen.

GROWTH GUIDE

The baby's small and primitive heart has started to beat vigorously with each passing day, and brainwave activity can be detected. The baby is now called an **embryo**. Between weeks three and six, red blood cells are being formed by the **yolk sac**, a provisional structure in charge of producing blood until Baby's placenta, liver, **thymus** and **bone marrow** are capable of carrying out this task. Two delicate yet firm layers compose the amniotic sac. This sac envelops the embryo and isolates him/her from the uterine surroundings (e.g., noise, light, thumps, etc.). These layers firmly bind and form the umbilical cord that will connect the placenta to the baby. All the structures of the new being now measure only one inch in diameter, while the embryo is merely four to five milimeters. [Note: Medical data in reference to size and weight of the baby during early pregnancy varies greatly. The author's data is based on "fertilization weeks" as opposed to "menstrual weeks."]

Week Five...

> *You watched me as I was being formed in utter seclusion.*
>
> *Psalm 139:15*

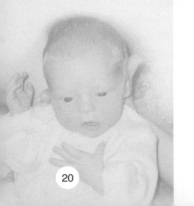

Hi, Mom! At some point during this week, I have become an embryo! If you could see me now, you would notice that I already have a small head. Even my brain and spine are beginning to develop at this stage. Although you can't see me yet, it is reassuring to know that our Creator God is monitoring my development, shaping me into one of His unique creations.

Mommy, thanks for nourishing yourself

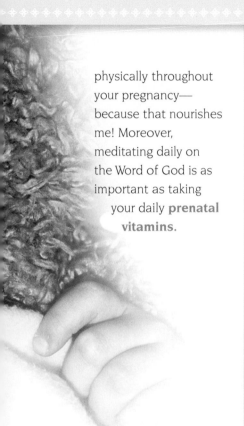

physically throughout your pregnancy— because that nourishes me! Moreover, meditating daily on the Word of God is as important as taking your daily **prenatal vitamins.**

Mom's Response:

Heavenly Father, I am learning anew that You are truly a God of mind-boggling details! What a powerful yet loving Creator You are! No wonder the psalmists ascribe all praise and glory to You! Amen.

GROWTH GUIDE

The embryo has adopted a C-shaped curvature measuring ten to twelve milimeters, about the size of an apple seed. The heart and its protective lining, called the **pericardium**, are prominent and occupy most of the available space. The nervous tissue is organized into sections called **somites,** which then form muscles, bones and the nerves of the trunk.

During this time arm and leg buds are forming and little digital ridges indicate future fingers. The embryo is now floating in a fluid-filled sac as the umbilical cord continues to develop. During this time the thyroid gland and special outgrowths from the belly become visible. The embryo has the beginning of the digestive system. The stomach and chest are developing as well as the liver, the pancreas and the gall bladder. The baby's little mouth and jaw are now noticeable.

Every moment

you know

where I am.

Psalm 139:3

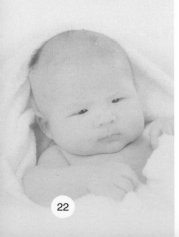

$\mathcal{M}$om, it's kind of embarrassing to say, but one-half of my body is my head! On it you can see the rough features of my face. My ears and other senses are also forming in synchronization with my brain. All of them are important parts of my body because they will become my windows to the world. Through them I will express my thoughts, emotions and will. God is crafting me to become a loving and caring person. Mommy, please teach me to use all my senses to enjoy nature and to always give thanks to God for creating it.

GROWTH GUIDE

During this time the baby's head is relatively large compared to the rest of the body. The embryo measures one inch (twenty-five milimeters) and weighs close to one gram. The face is forming and is becoming progressively visible. Eyes begin as black pigment dots on each side of the head. Traces of optic nerve and eye structures also become present. Meanwhile the ears and nasal organs are forming. The muscles that support the face, neck and throat, as well as the **mandible** and the **hyoid bone,** will begin to appear. The newly forming lungs begin to connect to the throat through the **bronchial tubes.**

Mom's Response:

O Lord, I am just now beginning to understand the enormous love You must possess to be able to embrace the whole world with Your divine love. Certainly, Your love surpasses all others! Amen.

23

Week Seven ...

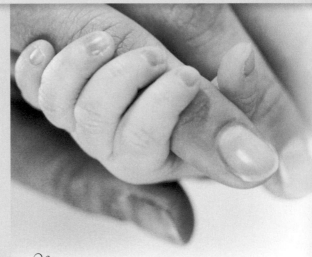

You know when I sit down or stand up. You know my every thought when far away.

Psalm 139:2

ℳom, you aren't able to feel it yet, but I've begun to move my little arms and legs. Soon I'll be jumping with infinite freedom inside my house! You are probably feeling just the opposite—sleepy and prone to rest. This is God's way of slowing you down while intense creative activity is going on inside of you. Did you know that between weeks four and eight my size will increase ten times?

In addition to feeling tired, you might also be feeling a bit queasy due to the great amount of hormones released in your body. Here's a tip: Try to eat small amounts several times a day in order to control the feeling of nausea and heartburn.

Mom's Response:

Dear Lord, thank You for showing me that these small physical discomforts are really insignificant when compared to the tremendous creative forces at work inside my body. Thank You for helping me cope with all of these new experiences. Amen.

GROWTH GUIDE

The embryo can now be called a **fetus,** which means "young one," and is 30 milimeters long, about the size of a large grape. The arms and legs are clearly visible, with clefts at the end that will become fingers and toes. At this time bone cells are beginning to develop. The baby's intestines, which were forming on the exterior along with the umbilical cord, begin to interiorize. The kidneys have begun to develop, and the urinary and rectal passages are separated but not yet open to the exterior. Special **endocrine glands** are beginning to function. The outline of the baby's nervous system is nearly complete. At this time the baby will start to move.

Week Eight...

I will pour out my Spirit and my blessings on your children.

Isaiah 44:3

𝑀om, if you want me to have a great smile for our future family photo albums, it is important for you to be taking an adequate supply of calcium on a daily basis.

Families are part of God's master plan to ensure that knowledge of His love and care for us is passed on from one generation to the next. That's why this is a good time to tighten family ties and to discover the roots and branches of our extended family. It's also a good time to thank God for family members who have modeled a godly lifestyle and to pray for those family members who have not met their Creator yet.

Mom's Response:

Dear Lord, thank You for this little one who will begin a new generation of our family. Teach me how to raise this child to honor and obey You. I pray that our family chain will be faithful to pass on Your love and care in tangible ways. Amen.

GROWTH GUIDE

During this time period, as the brain develops, the baby's head grows in immense proportions. The face becomes more and more recognizable. Facial clefts have closed, the nose seems to have a tip, the nostrils have formed and the two sides of the jaw have joined to make a mouth. The tongue has also formed. The heart can now circulate blood around the fetus. The baby's heartbeat can be clearly heard with the aid of the **Doppler. Ultrasound** allows you to see the baby inside the embryonic sac and his/her heart beating vigorously. The baby's sexual organs are inside the body but are not yet fully formed. The fetus now measures forty milimeters and weighs two grams.

27

Week Nine...

*When **I** look at the night sky and see the work of your fingers ... what are mortals that you should think of us?*

Psalm 8:3-4

$\mathcal{M}$om, our Father God cares about every aspect of our total development—physical, emotional and spiritual. I'm not only growing physically by leaps and bounds, but God has also given me emotions and spiritual awareness. I can only imagine that your emotions must be on a roller-coaster ride! Hang on, Mom, because God has promised never to leave us or forsake us. Praise Him!

Mom's Response:

Loving heavenly Father, it's a privilege to have direct communication with the Creator of the universe. Help me to control my emotions during these next months and enable me to give spiritual encouragement to my family and friends. Amen.

GROWTH GUIDE

The inner parts of the baby's ears, responsible for balance and hearing, are forming. **Ossification** begins from the skull downward, starting at the **occipital bone,** down the jaws, the **clavicle** and the long bones of the superior and inferior extremities respectively. The arms and legs have grown longer, and shoulders, elbows, hips and knees are detectable. The fingers and toes are becoming more distinct, though they are joined by webs of skin. Fingerprints are becoming progressively evident.

Week Ten...

I know that you can do anything, and no one can stop you.

Job 42:2

𝓜ommy, my growth has been relentless. It's amazing that in fewer than seventy days I have progressed from being a cell the size of a pinhead to a small person almost totally formed. I am composed of millions of cells—each one of them with specific form and function! How can anyone deny God's active participation in our creation?

Mommy, I want you and Daddy to teach me all about God when I grow up. In fact, you can start singing to me about Him now, and I'll soon be able to hear you!

Mom's Response:

*Dear Lord, in order
for me to be a good
teacher, I have to
be well prepared.
Father, continue to
reveal Yourself to me
through Your Word
and by Your Holy
Spirit. Amen.*

GROWTH GUIDE

The baby now measures eight centimeters and weighs fifteen grams, revealing the incredible rate of growth. Within the last two months the baby's size has grown by a factor of 40. The lungs and heart are individually isolated by a special lining. Inside the baby's chest, heart and lungs are also surrounded by individual air chambers, which allow their unrestricted movement for a lifelong period.

At this time fingernails and toenails begin to appear. Teeth are also beginning to form. The nervous system is still functioning at a primitive level, limited to reflex responses and involuntary movements. Baby's bone marrow begins to form.

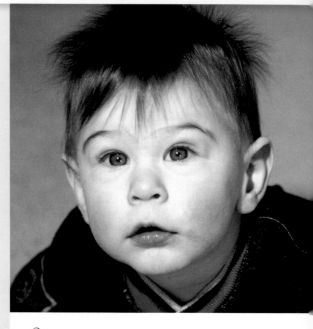

*Jesus grew
both in
height and in
wisdom, and
he was loved
by God and
by all who
knew him.*

Luke 2:52

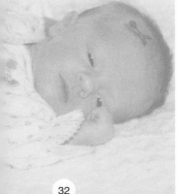

*M*ommy, did you know that right about now I'm a complete human being about the size of your thumb? All my members and organs have already formed. From now on all I need is to grow and mature.

Mommy, when I grow up, I would like to be as brave as you and as strong as Daddy. I'm also going to ask you lots of questions about your own childhood. Maybe between naps you can put together a scrapbook for me to look at while I sit in your lap!

Mom's Response:

Dear Lord, it is reassuring—and humbling—to know that You came to earth and experienced birth and childhood. You know what it's like to live in this world. Help me to train up my child in the way he should go. Amen.

GROWTH GUIDE

The mother should limit the intake of caffeine-containing foods (coffee, cola-type soft drinks, chocolate and black tea). The placenta filters blood in order to protect the baby, but caffeine is one of the substances that can pass through this barrier. Excessive caffeine consumption has been related to low birth weight and sleep problems of babies. Likewise, caffeine is related to higher levels of cholesterol and loss of calcium in mothers. Therefore, diets must include vitamin D and calcium-rich foods such as milk and other **dairy products**. Corn tortillas, dry grains and sardines are other good sources of calcium. Vitamin D promotes the transport and absorption of calcium to the bones and teeth for both the mother and the developing fetus.

> **D**o not be
> afraid, for **I**
> have ransomed
> you. **I** have
> called you by
> name; you
> are mine.
>
> Isaiah 43:1

Mom, this week I have fingerprints outlined on my hands and feet. You can also see the contour of my nose, lips and chin. I'm taking on my own identity! In the loving eyes of Father God, I am a unique and precious masterpiece, a priceless, original work, created to accomplish a specific and eternal purpose.

Mommy, as you and Daddy begin to discuss what my name will be, it's

GROWTH GUIDE

The baby's eyelids have developed and keep the eyes covered. The baby has earlobes. He can curl and fan his toes. He can move the muscles of his lips and open and close his mouth. He can suck, and he swallows amniotic fluid. He can even urinate. Ultrasound reveals the baby's facial features, heartbeat, leg movements and gender.

amazing to think that my heavenly Father has already assigned a name for me that expresses His plan for my life.

Mom's Response:

Almighty God, I cannot fathom the immensity of Your greatness. You know intimately every person who was ever born. You have a name and a purpose for each one. O Lord, I pray now that this little child within me will come to know Your greatness at a very early age. Amen.

Week Thirteen...

Nothing in all creation will ever be able to separate us from the love of God.

Romans 8:39

$\mathcal{M}$ommy, your breasts are getting ready to be my best food source. They will provide preventive medicine for future stress. Please don't allow anyone to put baby bottles or pacifiers in my mouth during the first month. It might cause **nipple confusion** and I will reject your milk, which was wisely and lovingly designed for me by our heavenly Father. In your breasts I will find consolation and

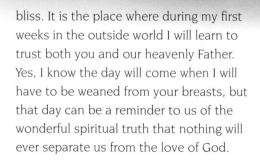

bliss. It is the place where during my first weeks in the outside world I will learn to trust both you and our heavenly Father. Yes, I know the day will come when I will have to be weaned from your breasts, but that day can be a reminder to us of the wonderful spiritual truth that nothing will ever separate us from the love of God.

GROWTH GUIDE

The baby's bones have now started to generate his/her own blood, which will be kept separate from your own bloodstream. The placenta serves as a multiple barrier: It allows the passing of oxygen, **nutrients** and **antibodies** while filtering residue and keeping many toxic substances out of the baby's bloodstream. Unfortunately, substances such as nicotine, alcohol, drugs and toxins aren't filtered, and they can affect the baby's development and maturing. In case you do not know your **blood type** yet, it is advisable to order a blood test. If you happen to be **Rh negative** your doctor will advise you if you need to take a special vaccine by the end of your pregnancy.

Mom's Response:

Loving heavenly Father, I can sense many amazing changes occurring in my body. You are truly a wonderful Creator. Thank You that You care for each one of Your precious children. Amen.

Week Fourteen...

With his love, he will calm all your fears. He will exult over you by singing a happy song.

Zephaniah 3:17

*M*om, I feel happier by the day in my lukewarm home, and I can express it with a smiling face! I react when I hear the sound of your voice. How much I enjoy listening to you sing or share your future dreams with me.

Sing me lullabies, tell me stories and let me listen to your laughter. But even more importantly, read to me often from the Bible, because it is the true source of wisdom for all of God's children.

Mom's Response:

Dear God, is it true that You are singing a happy song on my behalf today? What a privilege it is for me to go through this journey with You constantly by my side! Amen.

GROWTH GUIDE

The baby already measures six inches and weighs over two ounces. His internal organs are slowly beginning to function. The baby is very active inside the womb and reacts instinctively to external stimulation, especially to sound. His heartbeats sound like the "choo-choo" of a train but run at twice the speed of the mother's heart. His heartbeat frequency increases upon sudden excitement or danger. Baby makes breathing movements with his chest. He can suck his thumb.

Above all else, guard your heart, for it affects everything you do.

Proverbs 4:23

$\mathcal{M}$om, you and Daddy have a pretty big job ahead of you as you try to raise me in a wayward world. I hope you will teach me that my **sexuality** is a sacred gift from God. Help me to choose **abstinence** as the best prevention against the many things that could harm my happiness, my health and my future. When you pray for me, pray also for my future spouse. It's not too soon to start!

Mom's Response:

Dear God, my child is going to grow up in a confused world with conflicting values. Help me to be a responsible teacher, but please guard the heart of my child by Your divine power. Amen.

Sexual differentiation is complete. The ovaries of girls contain follicles, which means that you are already carrying the seed of your future grandchildren. The baby grows rapidly during this month. His/Her skin is so thin that it is transparent, and networks of blood vessels can be seen underneath. During this week the baby starts the development of adipose tissue (fatty tissue) in his body.

Morning sickness may stop and your appetite will increase; this is why you are also gaining weight fast: Up to nine pounds are considered normal by this time. Your regular clothes will probably be too tight, but you are not ready for maternity clothes yet.

You do not belong to yourself, for God bought you with a high price. So you must honor God with your body.

1 Corinthians 6:19-20

𝔐 om, some of the bodily discomforts you've felt during the past few months have subsided. But now you have a hearty appetite! Let's show off and enjoy your pregnancy! What about walking outdoors or starting a routine of gentle exercise? This will put you in good shape for the physical demands of **labor** and childbirth. Our Creator God gave us marvelous bodies, but we're the ones who need to maintain them. Thank you for setting a good example for me and others.

Mom's Response:

Dear God, I have to admit that I'm a little slower and a bit self-conscious with my changing shape. Help me to be more disciplined in the care of my body. Thank You. Amen.

GROWTH GUIDE

You continue to put on weight. By this week you may have gained between nine and thirteen pounds, but only four ounces actually correspond to the baby! It is time to start a daily routine of exercise in order to achieve the physical fitness needed later. Walking or swimming is excellent exercise for pregnant women.

The baby's eyebrows and eyelashes are growing, and he is developing fine downy hair known as **lanugo** on his face and body. Joints have formed in his arms and legs, and hard bones are developing. The baby moves around vigorously, but you are not able to feel him yet.

Week Seventeen...

And the LORD God formed a man's body from the dust of the ground and breathed into it the breath of life. And the man became a living person.

Genesis 2:7

$\mathcal{M}$om, this week my body is rehearsing over and over again the routine functions it will perform for a lifetime. I breathe and swallow far better now. Every breath I take is a reminder to me that I am made in the image of God, because God first breathed life into man. Thank you, Mommy, that you will bring me up in a home that fears and respects the almighty God.

Mom's Response:

Dear God, at times I feel so inadequate to raise my child in a way that will be pleasing to You. I hope You don't mind, but I'll be coming to You pretty often to ask for Your advice! Amen.

GROWTH GUIDE

The baby's digestive, urinary and genital tubes open to the exterior at the **perineum**.

Meanwhile, the placenta filters blood—almost seventy-five gallons each day—and completely renews the baby's blood every thirty seconds. The placenta controls most of the vital functions of the baby until the moment he can perform them by himself. By the time the baby is due, the placenta will have grown old. The kidneys are working, and the bladder discharges "innocent" urine into the amniotic fluid. Waste does not build up because the amniotic fluid is renewed continuously.

Not even a sparrow, worth only half a penny, can fall to the ground without your Father knowing it. And the very hairs on your head are all numbered.

Matthew 10:29-30

$\mathcal{M}$om . . . guess what? I've got hair growing on my head! And I'm sure you'd love to know what color it is. It's pretty normal for you to have lots of questions right now: How many weeks left until my arrival? What day will I be born? When will I sleep through the night? Do you have everything you need for my care? When is the last day you should work?

Take it easy, Mom. God is in control, and He has told us not to worry about anything. So, trust Him, Mom, and enjoy the rest of your pregnancy. I sure will!

Mom's Response:

O Lord, why is it so easy to lose sight of You when You are so faithful to me? And why is it more natural for me to worry than to trust You? Lord, I want You to make Your presence very real in my life. Amen.

GROWTH GUIDE

The baby is very active, especially after the mother has eaten **carbohydrate**-rich foods. You may even feel his first kicks and movements. The baby's body is now completely covered by lanugo—evidence that the skin has almost finished its development. The growth of your womb has stretched the skin and muscles of your belly, so it is not uncommon to feel some itching. Apply **humectant** creams or gel with vitamins A and E.

Week Nineteen...

Don't you know that your body is the temple of the **Holy Spirit,** *who lives in you and was given to you* **by God?**

1 Corinthians 6:19

$\mathcal{M}$ommy, how can anyone say that our bodies are the result of some random evolutionary development? God has made us so complex, it is almost mind-boggling. The divine design of our human bodies is perfect. I want to learn how to take care of it by keeping myself away from any contamination that could harm it, such as alcohol or drugs. I want to make you smile with my pure, natural, God-given joy!

Mom's Response:

Dear God, I pray that my child will always respect the body You are forming. Help me provide the proper nourishment needed to develop a strong and healthy child. Amen.

GROWTH GUIDE

The skin of the baby is still translucent because it does not have enough fat underneath. Your skin, on the other hand, is now more sensitive and is prone to pigmentation: Moles and freckles may darken noticeably. Your nipples and surrounding skin may darken, and a dark line may appear down the center of your abdomen, but it will fade after birth.

It is normal to feel a slight swelling in your lower legs by the end of the day. Do not cross your legs or use tight stockings. When you sit, try to keep your legs at the same level or higher than your body. This way you can prevent **varicose veins** and the swelling of your feet.

Week Twenty...

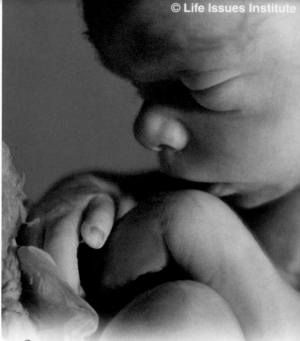

Create in me a clean heart, O God. Renew a right spirit within me.

Psalm 51:10

*M*om, my heartbeats can be heard distinctly by you and your doctors. God can hear my heart beating too, and it brings Him such joy that another new life will be brought into His world. As our heavenly Father, He wants His children to have clean hearts. He wants our motives to be pure so He can use us for His honor and glory.

I can feel your heart beating, Mommy. Is it clean?

Mom's Response:

Dear Lord, I want to be a clean vessel before You. I know that You are a holy and righteous God and that I am a sinner. Please forgive my sins so that I may grow closer to You. Amen.

GROWTH GUIDE

The baby weighs ten ounces and measures nine inches. Your uterus is also growing and has reached the level of your belly button. Pregnancy brings an important increase in the blood volume of your body, so you will need additional liquid intake. Feeling thirsty is normal at this time. Drink at least eight glasses of water every day instead of soft drinks, and eat whole fruits instead of juice drinks. Good nutrition must be
- balanced (including all food groups)
- complete (sufficient daily servings)
- adequate (meeting your personal needs)

Eating small meal **portions** several times a day and avoiding food just before going to bed will prevent heartburn and improve digestion.

Week Twenty-One...

Don't worry about having enough food or drink or clothing ... Your heavenly Father already knows all your needs.

Matthew 6:31-32

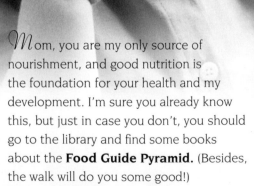

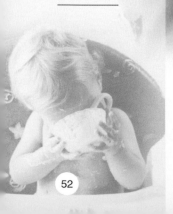

ℳom, you are my only source of nourishment, and good nutrition is the foundation for your health and my development. I'm sure you already know this, but just in case you don't, you should go to the library and find some books about the **Food Guide Pyramid.** (Besides, the walk will do you some good!)

Not only do we need to fill our bodies

Protective grease called **vernix** starts to cover the baby this week. It protects his/her skin and lubricates the passage through the **birth canal.**

At this point of pregnancy, you may have noticed red marks on your skin; they are stretch lines called **striae.** Weight gain, dryness of the skin and skin quality can influence the severity of the stretch marks. Also, eating processed foods that contain chemicals and salt may increase your liquid retention and the likelihood of swelling.

with the right kinds of food, we also need to feed our minds and souls with spiritual nourishment. Mom, have you read any good books lately? Have you read any of "The Book" lately?

Mom's Response:

Dear God, there's so much about You that I don't know. Help me to find time to study Your Word and to apply it to my life. Amen.

Week Twenty-Two...

As the clay is in the potter's hand, so are you in my hand.

Jeremiah 18:6

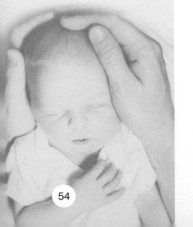

Mom, did you know that after I am born your milk is the only food I need during my first six months? Its composition is adjusted daily according to my needs. By our loving Creator's design, breast-feeding is the most practical thing for both of us. You will recover your shape faster and reduce your risk of developing breast cancer. The most special thing, however, is that breast-feeding creates a wonderful bond between you and me. It will give me the sense of security needed to succeed and walk confidently in life.

Mom's Response:

Thank You, Lord, for creating me with everything I need to bring this little one into the world. I am seeing now how so much of what is happening to my baby and me is the sovereign outworking of a plan already set in motion by a Master Designer. I praise You, Father. Amen.

GROWTH GUIDE

The baby has reached the one-pound mark. His/Her body is reaching the right proportions, and the hands have developed unique wrinkles.

Your breasts have increased in size and are preparing for lactation. Your milk is easy to digest and prevents infections and allergies. It contains antibodies (to protect the baby from diseases) and exclusive nutrients that promote optimal development of the human brain and many more organs.

> *God has made everything beautiful for its own time.*
>
> *Ecclesiastes 3:11*

$\mathcal{M}$om, as you are waiting for the big day, take time now to prepare physically and emotionally for your labor and my delivery. That day will be one you will never forget, and God is already making the necessary adjustments inside your body to ensure that I will make my grand entrance without a hitch.

As important as it will be for me to enter your world, Mom, it's even more important that we will be ready to enter our eternal home. I hope that "God" will become a household word in our family. I want to learn all about Him and His great love.

GROWTH GUIDE

Your baby's skin is reddish and thin. His or her legs have elongated by thirty percent during the past month. The baby now weighs almost one and a half pounds—that is six times the weight two months ago and twice the weight one month ago! He/She is suspended in the amniotic fluid, which plays a very important role during pregnancy because it

- protects the baby against impact and noise;
- allows the pilot testing of swallowing, breathing and digesting;
- regulates temperature;
- provides an environment for free movement.

Mom's Response:

Dear Lord, there are already so many preparations to make this big change about to happen in my life. Don't allow these things to get in the way of my relationship with You. Amen.

*Perfect love
expels all
fear.*

1 John 4:18

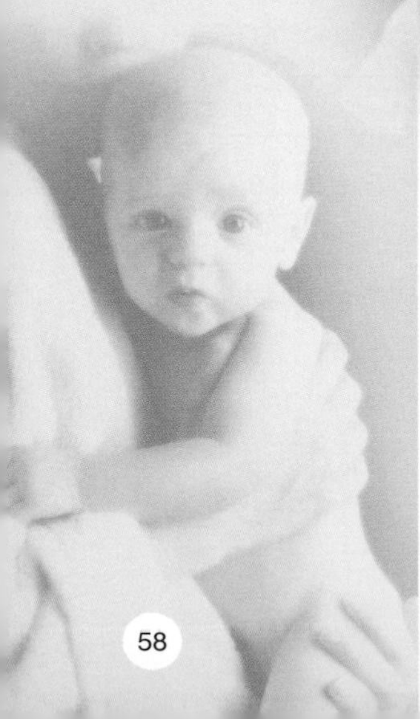

$\mathcal{M}$om, it's possible that you are experiencing occasional nightmares because of hormonal changes, or maybe you move quickly from joy to tears. You also may be more vulnerable to fear and pain. Fortunately, you will return to your normal self after you give birth to me. But these fluctuations in your emotions can serve as good reminders for you to

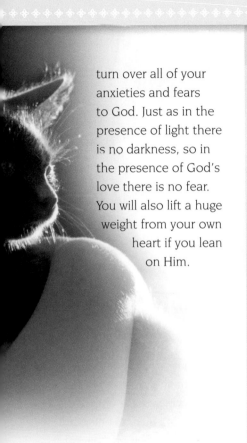

turn over all of your anxieties and fears to God. Just as in the presence of light there is no darkness, so in the presence of God's love there is no fear. You will also lift a huge weight from your own heart if you lean on Him.

Mom's Response:

Dear Lord, help me to let go of my fears and to place my burdens in Your arms. Thank You for Your willingness to carry them for me. Amen.

You may realize that now you sweat more frequently and feel warmer. This is caused by the increase in blood irrigation and the action of hormones.

By this time the baby is developing sweat glands beneath the skin. He moves frequently but also takes rest periods. If you perceive any significant change in his movement patterns, discuss it with your doctor. Your baby frowns. Sudden or strong noises wake him up. Some babies even prefer certain types of music.

All praise to the God and Father of our Lord Jesus Christ. He is the source of every mercy and the God who comforts us. He comforts us in all our troubles.

2 Corinthians 1:3-4

*M*om, we're about to begin our sixth month together! I'm already thirteen inches long! This is a time when some unexpected events may happen at any moment, but it gives me peace to know that my heavenly Father is as loving as He is powerful. His mercy and faithfulness have no end. He has assigned an eternal purpose to each life no matter how brief it is, and for those of us who are united to Him, everything works together for our good, no matter how unexpected it might be.

Mom's Response:

Dear God, help me to cope with the range of emotions that I will soon begin to experience. Help me to be patient and loving to my friends and loved ones. Give me an extra dose of Your comfort. Amen.

GROWTH GUIDE

Your **uterine height** has reached eight inches (almost three inches above your belly button). By now you look truly pregnant. This month could be described as the "perfect month" of pregnancy: The risk of miscarriage is very low, and the baby could survive birth with special care. The movements of your baby sometimes cause intense but not painful sensations, which can be soothed by resting on your left side. If you experience continued pain, you should discuss it with your doctor.

You will keep in perfect peace all who trust in you, whose thoughts are fixed on you!

Isaiah 26:3

$\mathcal{M}$ommy, today I was awakened by a new and funny sensation: It is called **hiccups** and makes me kick you with more rhythm than usual. Sorry, Mom, for waking you as well. But if my hiccupping doesn't awaken you, your sudden cravings probably will. Your appetite is hearty right now, but you may have noticed

that your digestion has slowed down. That's pretty natural, because your hormones are already beginning to prepare your body for childbirth.

Mommy, your inner peacefulness will help me tremendously during these last

several weeks as you keep your mind focused on God and His love for you.

Mom's Response:

Dear Lord, this will be a time of physical and emotional stretching for me. Please flood my soul with Your peace. Amen.

GROWTH GUIDE

After twenty-six weeks your body weight will have increased approximately eighteen pounds. It is not just your belly: Your whole body also looks fuller. Your baby's body also begins to look rounder, thanks to the accumulation of fat underneath his skin.

You may be feeling more flexible and relaxed due to the production of a hormone called **relaxin,** which keeps your uterus relaxed and makes your pelvic joints more flexible in preparation for labor. This hormone also makes your intestines work slower and your bladder work faster.

For the Spirit of God has made me, and the breath of the Almighty gives me life.

Job 33:4

𝓜ommy, my lungs are maturing day by day. This is important because as soon as my lungs are ready to breathe on their own, the labor process will begin. How exciting!

As I wait patiently for my heavenly Father to complete His work of creating me, my only companion in the seclusion of your womb is the beating of your heart. I am so thankful to God that He has given me a loving mother to nurture me through these wonderful days of my development. I want to remember this intimacy forever!

Mom's Response

Dear Lord, sometimes when I think of the responsibility of raising this child within me, I get overwhelmed. How will I know what to do and when to do it? Please stay close to me, heavenly Father. I need Your divine guidance. You are the eternal parent. Amen.

GROWTH GUIDE

The baby is growing fast. He now weighs over two pounds, and he measures between twelve and fourteen inches. You are gaining weight as well, and from now on you will gain one half pound per week. By the end of your pregnancy, your initial weight will have increased by about twenty-eight pounds.

Your uterus is pushing up your **diaphragm** and lungs, forcing them to breathe faster in order to oxygenate both your blood and the baby's. The baby's lungs are not yet fully developed. They have been covered internally with a soapy substance called **surfactant** that prevents them from collapsing during breathing. Once the lungs have matured, they will send a signal to your brain, instructing it to liberate **oxytocin** or "birth hormone."

Week Twenty-Eight...

You have taught children and nursing infants to give you praise.

Psalm 8:2

Mom, I can now blink with my new eyelids, and I can now hear perfectly well. If you talk to me often and call me by my new name, I will learn to respond to it. Tell me often how much you love me—I love to hear your voice. It is very soothing to me.

Our heavenly Father wants us to talk often with Him. He not only wants to hear our prayer requests, but He also wants to hear from our lips how much we love and trust Him. Mommy, will you take a moment and praise Him now? He loves to hear our voices as much as I love to hear yours!

Mom's Response:

Dear heavenly Father, forgive me for being so wrapped up in my own needs that I often neglect to spend quality time with You. Teach me, Lord, to slow down enough to hear Your voice even in the midst of my busy days. I praise You, Lord. Amen.

GROWTH GUIDE

The membrane that protected the baby's eyes has disappeared; your baby can now blink. By this time the brain begins to develop its characteristic grooves and wrinkles, allowing it to perceive complex perceptions and reactions. The baby can now taste, listen and react to pain and external stimulation.

Try to keep your backbone straight in order to prevent back pain, especially when lifting objects. It is time to start practicing the **Kegel exercises** to strengthen the **pelvic floor muscles.** This is important for sexual pleasure, preventing urine leaks and for **pushing** effectively during labor.

3

4

5

6

7

8

9

10

11

12

13

Week Twenty-Nine...

For I know the plans I have for you.... They are plans for good and not for disaster, to give you a future and a hope.

Jeremiah 29:11

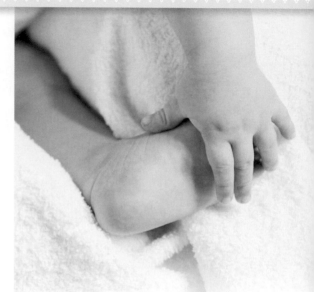

Mom, I'm really having fun experimenting with my arms and legs. You might think I spend all my time floating around and sucking my thumb. But pretty soon I'll be practicing my soccer kick! So I hope you're making plans for that great day. Remember, Mom, this will be our personal and special event, so it's important for you to make informed decisions.

I'm grateful, too, that our heavenly Father has already made His wonderful plans for my life. I can't wait to see what He has in store for us!

Mom's Response:

O Lord, the future seems like such a long distance from now. But with You by my side, I can confidently take it a day at a time. Thank You for Your faithfulness. Amen.

GROWTH GUIDE

By this time of pregnancy, you will begin to experience some slight discomforts, such as indigestion, heartburn or cramps. Also, the movements of your baby within you are now evident.

As the delivery date approaches, you should educate yourself on the various delivery options. Do you prefer a physician or **midwife**? Hospital, maternity center or in-home childbirth? Natural, **anesthesia** or **underwater birth? Medical intervention** or not? Breast-feed or bottle-feed with **formula**?

A good start for you is to prearrange visits to different health providers. Bring some written questions, share your plans with the person in charge of your childbirth and ask about his/her record of medical interventions during deliveries, his/her position in regard to abortion and his/her **birth philosophy.**

Week Thirty...

He will carry the lambs in his arms, holding them close to his heart. He will gently lead the mother sheep with their young.

Isaiah 40:11

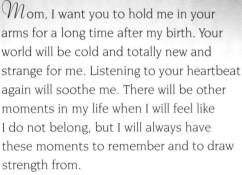

Mom, I want you to hold me in your arms for a long time after my birth. Your world will be cold and totally new and strange for me. Listening to your heartbeat again will soothe me. There will be other moments in my life when I will feel like I do not belong, but I will always have these moments to remember and to draw strength from.

Mommy, try to get as much rest as you can. You may feel alone sometimes, but you have a loving Shepherd ready to help you along the way.

GROWTH GUIDE

The baby has reached the three-pound mark and measures almost fifteen inches. He/She is running out of space to maneuver freely, so the baby slowly begins to accommodate for the delivery position (head down).

Slight insomnia is normal for the mother at this stage; however, if you are not used to sleeping on your side, it is time to practice because soon it will ensure a better night's sleep.

Mom's Response:

Loving Shepherd, guide me to safe pastures and cool streams. Thank You for carrying me when I lose my way or when the storm clouds threaten. Amen.

Week Thirty-One...

Children are a gift from the LORD; they are a reward from him.

Psalm 127:3

$\mathcal{M}$om, tell me about Daddy! Although he may not know it, my present and future stability will depend a lot on his participation in my early life.

Love him much, Mom. He might be feeling a little displaced by me because of all the attention I am demanding right now. Honor him and pray for him to be obedient to the guidance of our heavenly Father. Daddy has been given the great role of mentor and shepherd of our home. Through his godly leadership our family will receive our share of God's blessing and prosperity.

Mommy, tell Daddy that I love him and can't wait to feel the stubble on his chin!

Mom's Response:

O Lord, I pray for my husband. Help him to always look to You and Your Word for daily guidance. Bless him as he takes on this added responsibility of being an earthly father. Be a mentor to Him, Father. Amen.

GROWTH GUIDE

By now you have gained approximately twenty-one pounds. Try to rest at least twice a day, raising your feet. Continue to get good nutrition. It's still good to have five or six small meals every day as opposed to three heavy ones. Limit the daily intake of carbs to three servings per meal and a maximum of eleven per day. Gaining weight is a natural part of pregnancy, and much of the weight will come off after labor and lactation. If you are overweight, it is better to exercise more rather than skip meals.

Keep practicing the Kegel exercises, and remember that prenatal vitamins do not replace food.

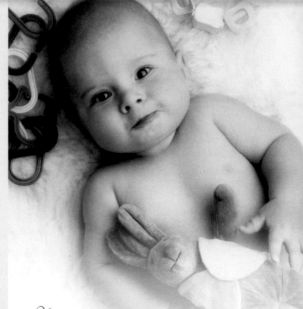

> *As for God, his way is perfect. All the LORD's promises prove true.*
>
> *2 Samuel 22:31*

$\mathcal{M}$om, this is a good time to start making practical preparations for my arrival—like getting things in order at the office, packing your hospital suitcase and preparing my bedroom. I'm anxious to see what colors you've selected!

By now it should be obvious that I will be coming soon. God's plans for me from before the foundation of time will soon be revealed. Mommy, my birth isn't just a natural event; it is a sacred act because of God's divine participation. His way is always perfect, and His promises are always fulfilled. What a marvelous heavenly Father is watching over us during these days and for all time!

Mom's Response:

Dear loving Father, it is awesome to think that Your thoughts toward my child have existed since eternity past. This is a lot for me to comprehend. Help me to see more clearly Your perfect, divine hand in every aspect of my life. I want always to be aware of Your presence. Amen.

GROWTH GUIDE

Now is a good time to start your prenatal classes. Take time to choose one meeting your expectations. **Lamaze** prenatal classes will help you prepare for Baby's arrival. You will learn to make informed decisions regarding medical care, to take responsible control of your health and to trust your inner ability to birth a child. You will also learn about other safe options and styles for having your baby, including your right to have a baby without medical interventions.

Week Thirty-Three...

In quietness and confidence is your strength.

Isaiah 30:15

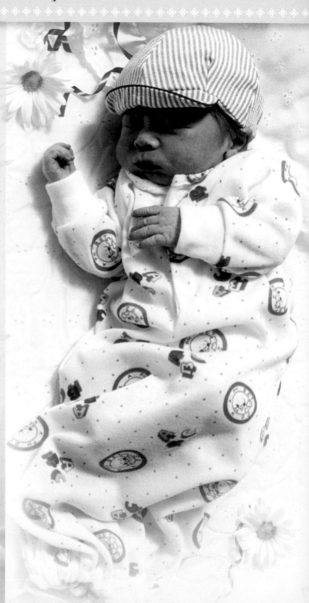

$\mathcal{M}$ommy, as soon as I'm born, the milk from your breasts will provide the perfect nourishment for my first days. While being held in your arms I will learn to trust as I look into your eyes and see your love for me. I will hear the comforting sound of your heart beating and your voice singing me lullabies. No matter how difficult or intimidating the world is, I will not be afraid because I am united with you. You may think breast-feeding is not very comfortable or convenient for you, but remember that it is God's chosen method of transitioning me into this new environment.

Mom's Response:

Heavenly Father, much of what is happening to me is beyond my control. Thank You that I have You to rely on for my strength and comfort. Lord, this child I will bear is Your creation. Enable me to raise him/her to Your honor and glory. Amen.

GROWTH GUIDE

Your breasts are ready to produce **colostrum** while the mature milk comes in. Breast milk is the perfect and sufficient food for the newborn baby. It is rich in antibodies and nutrients, and it contains the **laxative** the baby needs to clean the **meconium** from the intestines. The use of medication during labor and separating the baby from the mother delays the natural lactation process.

The movements of your baby are getting stronger each day; sometimes they can even cause painless **contractions** called **Braxton Hicks,** which disappear when you rest.

Week Thirty-Four...

Everyone who believes that Jesus is the Christ is a child of God. And everyone who loves the Father loves his children, too.

1 John 5:1

Mom, I love you. You are the most wonderful Mom to me despite the ailments and discomforts you might experience. Your gums may bleed after brushing, your bladder sends you urgent messages, your veins are dilated and your ankles and hands look swollen. Isn't pregnancy wonderful?

As you go through these trials, Daddy will be that special encourager you will need. He can help you to stay comfortable, and his tender glances of love will lift you up when you are not feeling so beautiful anymore. Your mutual love and trust will grow strong as you go through this challenging experience together. In the same way, as you and Daddy depend on the Lord during the trials of life, your love and trust in Him will strengthen as He continually proves His care for our family.

Mom's Response:

Dear Lord, I don't really like the idea of discomfort and pain. Please help me to manage it, as I would prefer not to use medicines during the birthing process. Lord, I feel a little guilty asking this of You, because I know that You experienced the worst kind of pain on my behalf. Thank You, Lord, for dying on the cross, for bearing my sins. I love You. Amen.

GROWTH GUIDE

As the end of pregnancy nears, anxiety about labor and pain may grow too intense for the future parents. Fear of the unknown is the most frequent source of stress, and stress intensifies pain. Prenatal classes and a childbirth plan help reduce anxiety as you learn natural strategies to break the vicious **cycle of pain.** Having a trained birth partner or hiring a **doula** can decrease by twenty-five to fifty percent the need for medicines and other medical interventions, such as anesthesia, **forceps**, **episiotomy** or **Cesarean section**. There is no reason for labor and delivery pain beyond what a healthy woman can naturally endure. Delivery pain is a different type of pain because it has rhythm, purpose and best of all, the gift of a new life.

> *Don't be
> afraid, for I
> am with you.
> Do not be
> dismayed, for
> I am your
> God.*
>
> Isaiah 41:10

𝓜ommy, if you know what to expect during my birth, you can respond appropriately and make it easier for both of us!

For example, be sure to practice different types of breathing. This will be useful to keep your mind busy and will ensure a good supply of oxygen for me. But don't think you have to deal with this all by yourself. Our Creator God has equipped you with a powerful natural analgesic called **endorphin** that is emitted after strong pain. Mommy, we have an awesome, caring God!

Mom's Response:

Dear God, the more I learn about my body and the baby I'm carrying, the more I am convinced of Your masterful, creative genius. It is beyond human comprehension. I praise You, my Creator, my Master, my Lord. Amen.

GROWTH GUIDE

You have gained twenty-four pounds, and your uterine height has reached twelve inches. The baby, who is now gaining about an ounce per day, looks much the same as he will at birth, but he still needs to fill out more. Inguinal rings have dilated in baby boys, and the testicles have descended.

The lack of space and the weight of the baby's head may have turned him/her into the correct position for birth. If you experience back pain, try resting on your hands and knees and leaning forward. This position, as opposed to lying flat in bed, helps prevent posterior presentation associated with painful and longer labors.

This is real love. It is not that we loved God, but that he loved us.

1 John 4:10

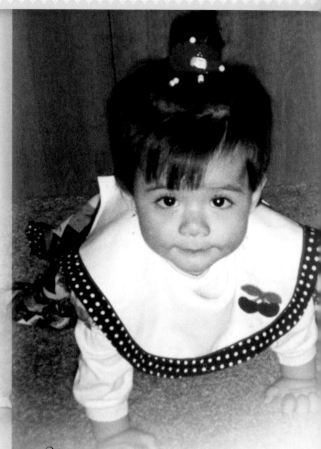

$\mathcal{M}$ommy, as we enter the ninth month together, the expectation of my arrival has captivated all those who know you. This month the waiting will seem very long— sometimes even uncomfortable—but never boring! You'll need a sense of humor, some regular exercise and lots of tender care from now on.

As you carry me through this last month, you need to remember that one of the reasons our heavenly Father sent His Son to earth was to help us overcome our fears. His perfect love drives away our fears! His love
is patient
  is kind
    always protects
     always trusts
    always hopes
     always perseveres
      and never ceases . . .
Mommy, this love is *for real*, and it's for us!

Mom's Response:

Dear Lord, as I face these last four weeks, I admit I am both afraid and excited at the same time. Fill me with Your perfect love so that there's no room for anxious thoughts. Amen.

GROWTH GUIDE

Some of the childbirth signals you will experience are descent of the womb, feeling lighter, bursts of energy, expulsion of the mucous plug, digestive changes, **breakage of the water** and, bottom line, the presence of regular contractions that are closer, longer and more intense. Childbirth has different **labor and delivery phases,** each with characteristic physical and emotional changes. Your mood will change as the process advances: Initially you will feel exhilarated and then more sober and self-centered.

How great is our Lord! His power is absolute! His understanding is beyond comprehension!

Psalm 147:5

Mom, please remember that I will also be in labor, moving through you, pushing out with my little head. Your inner being knows perfectly how to help me be born. Take courage from the fact that you have been beautifully and wonderfully created by God to be a mother and that everything has been arranged from the beginning of time for this moment.

The two of us are in the hands of an all-wise and all-powerful God. With His help, we cannot fail.

Mom's Response:

Dear Lord, so much of what is happening to me is outside of my control. I am obviously part of a relentless, miraculous process that You have built into Your astonishing creation. You are worthy to be praised. Amen.

GROWTH GUIDE

Labor can start at any moment. By now you should be visiting your health provider weekly. Medical personnel will evaluate your weight, uterine height and **blood pressure.** They will look for signs of **preeclampsia,** such as **albumin** in urine or **edema** in hands or feet during each visit. They will also check the baby's heart rate, position and movements.

Week Thirty-Eight...

Grandchildren are the crowning glory of the aged; parents are the pride of their children.

Proverbs 17:6

*M*om, I'm really proud of you! We've come all this way together and soon we'll be rubbing our noses together. Daddy coud cut my umbilical cord in order to introduce me to my new stand-alone life. Ask the doctor to allow this sacred moment. This is the moment when you and Daddy will officially become my parents—handpicked by God to bring me

up in the big world outside. You and Daddy have an important role as my new mentors once I am born. I am anxious to learn all about life from your collective experiences. Tell Daddy to put film in the camera— I'm coming soon!

Mom's Response:

Lord, You have been so faithful to me during this long journey. Some weeks I wasn't sure how I would make it through. But You have sustained me physically, emotionally and spiritually. Take my hand, Lord, and hold it tightly. Lead me gently through these next hours. Amen.

GROWTH GUIDE

Before the first phase of labor begins, you may experience irregular contractions that do not disappear with rest. You will feel them as pain that flows from your lower back forward and to the perineum. They may disappear or become more regular in duration, frequency and strength. Stay at home and continue sleeping if it is nighttime, or simply keep yourself busy with light duties. Light meals and frequent drinking will give you energy. When the contractions take place every ten minutes or less, you will spontaneously focus on yourself more and more. You can find relief in comfort measures such as taking a shower or bath, using a **birth ball** or a **rebozo.** Slow dancing or massage also helps labor. It will soon be time to call your doctor or midwife.

Week Thirty-Nine...

I will strengthen you. I will help you. I will uphold you with my victorious right hand.

Isaiah 41:10

Mommy, I'm all set to begin the final leg of my journey to my new home in the outside world. We are just down to days now. It will really help to keep your mind busy with phone conversations, letter writing, reading, small craft projects and prayer. God has been with us throughout this entire adventure—and He won't fail us now. In fact, it is in moments like these that God's presence will become especially noticeable. Mommy, in that final hour, search for the face of God and you will be comforted.

Mom's Response:

Dear heavenly Father, I take great comfort in knowing that You traveled a similar path when You made Your first appearance on this earth. Thank You, Lord, for understanding all of my needs as I go through these next hours. Please protect my child from any unseen dangers. Thank You. Amen.

GROWTH GUIDE

The climax of vulnerability, called **transition,** is reached just before full **dilation** of the **cervix.** This is the most intense and short stage, so you may feel uneasy and want to give up. You will need encouragement from those around you to reinforce your trust in your innate ability to give birth and to be reminded that the liberating final thrust is very near.

Pain is registered at the brain but qualified by the mind. The human body has its own way to face pain based on two physiological mechanisms: The first is called **chemical inhibition,** executed by releasing endorphins—powerful chemicals similar to morphine; the second mechanism uses neural and sensory signals to compete for your brain's attention **(Gate Control Theory).** Practice **breathing patterns** and **relaxation** techniques you learned in prenatal classes. These could keep your labor free of medications.

Week Forty...

$\mathcal{M}$om, we've made it to the last week! Don't get too antsy to go to the hospital—childbirth is a long process. Try to stay calm this week while your body does all the work. The ideal time to leave

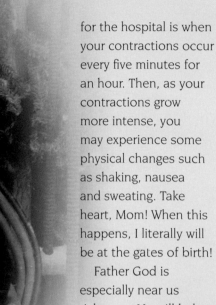

for the hospital is when your contractions occur every five minutes for an hour. Then, as your contractions grow more intense, you may experience some physical changes such as shaking, nausea and sweating. Take heart, Mom! When this happens, I literally will be at the gates of birth!

Father God is especially near us right now. He will help both of us manage the stresses we will undergo.

Mom's Response:

Dear Lord, You have promised that You would never leave us or forsake us. I claim that promise now and ask that You will flood me with Your perfect peace. Amen.

When your contractions occur every five minutes for more than an hour, you will likely turn irritable, confused and dependent. Expect the contractions to increase in frequency, intensity and duration. Dilation from eight to ten centimeters takes place quickly and could cause shaking, nausea, sweating and shivering. Don't be alarmed. This is a good sign that the baby is now descending the vaginal canal.

During the expulsive phase, pushing or blowing conscientiously in rhythm with your contractions will help the baby to get out safely. You can help your baby to descend faster by changing positions and by using the force of gravity to your advantage (keep your back in a vertical position). The baby's passage through the narrow vaginal canal activates his brain and squeezes his lungs, readying him for his first breath of air.

*It will be
like a woman
experiencing the
pains of labor.
When her child
is born, her
anguish gives
place to joy
because she has
brought a new
person into the
world.*

John 16:21

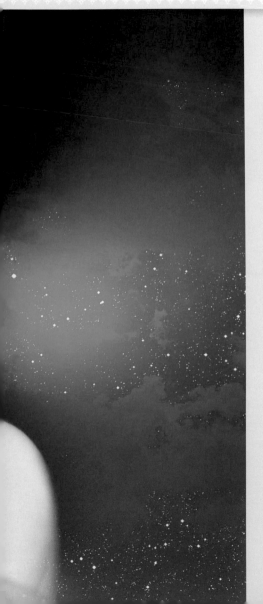

Mommy, today you will face the deepest and most encompassing event a human being can experience: childbirth. It will involve all your being: body, soul and spirit. The intensity of the pain will give way to the indescribable joy of holding me in your arms!

Mom, don't lose your focus now. Pain will soon pave the way to joy!

Mom's Response:

Dear Lord, Thank You for the miracle of new life. It is precious! Amen.

A Meditation for the Great Day

This will be a magnificent and most significant day, not only for your child but also for you. Today you have a divine appointment in the heavenly delivery room, because the Lord also wants to bless you with a new life. Just as a human baby must be born of a woman to inhabit his/her new earthly home, each of us must be "born again" spiritually to gain access to our heavenly home. Jesus said: "There are many rooms in my Father's home, and I am going to prepare a place for you" (John 14:2). Unfortunately, not everyone will see his/her new heavenly room. Why is this?

The first man and woman were created to have close fellowship with our Creator and heavenly Father. They were even made in His image and likeness (see Genesis 1:27). Sadly, however, Adam and Eve disobeyed God in the Garden of Eden, which resulted in both physical and spiritual death for the entire human race. Essentially, their "seed" has passed on from generation to generation.

Today we are still suffering the drastic consequences of that original sin. In fact, did you know that the pain you will experience in giving birth is a direct result of that first act of disobedience? (Read more about this in Genesis 3:16.)

However, the worst consequence of that original sin is that we are separated from the life of God. We are created "creatures" who are infected with sin and cannot have fellowship with a holy and righteous God. We sin by ignoring and disobeying God and by pursuing our own selfish interests. The Bible clearly states, "Because of your sin, he has turned away and will not listen anymore" (Isaiah 59:2).

Therefore, a provision needed to be made or else the entire human race would all be doomed to eternal separation from God.

Unbelievably, God Himself, out of His infinite mercy and love, provided the perfect rescue plan to guide us back to our heavenly home: "For God so loved the world that he gave his only Son, so that everyone who believes in him will not perish but have eternal life" (John 3:16).

Stripping Himself of His divine condition, God came down to this earth in the Person of Jesus Christ and experienced the extremities of human life from conception (see Luke 2:1-20) to death (see John 19). He did all of this out of love for you and me, all the while knowing the great cost it would be to Himself (see Romans 5:8). His pain, like yours, was originated in love and was intended to bring life.

God the Father offered His own sinless Son, Jesus Christ, as the only acceptable (i.e., perfect) sacrifice for our sins. Jesus, who died a terrible death on a cross, bore our sins so that we might have eternal life. Through Christ's death and resurrection, Christ gained the ultimate victory over sin and death. No more does sin need to reign in our lives. We have the promise of God's Holy Spirit to live pure, godly lives. He guides us, enables us and strengthens us to fulfill the wonderful purpose for which we were physically born. *We all are born to die some day, but Jesus died so that we could live eternally.*

While this wonderful provision has been made for us, we must intentionally accept this gift by faith. The Bible teaches that we can do *nothing* in and of ourselves to earn our salvation. Even if we are considered to be good and kind people, it will not pass muster because of the sinful nature we possess ("No one does good, not even one!" Psalm 53:3). Therefore, what is required according to the Scriptures is simply that if "you confess with your mouth that Jesus is Lord and believe in your heart that God raised him from the dead, you will be saved" (Romans 10:9).

By willingly trusting this provision for our own lives, we will be restored to our original identity and destiny: "But to all who believed him and accepted him, he gave the right to become children of God. They are reborn! This is not a physical birth resulting from human passion or plan—this rebirth comes from God" (John 1:12-13).

Thanks to Jesus Christ's atoning sacrifice of love, the broken communion with our heavenly Father has been completely restored. What an awesome provision!

Only our salvation gives meaning to the most beautiful story of love and sacrifice. Anything less than that is certainly a tragedy.

Today you will give birth to a baby. And today *you* can be born again too! Here is a summary of the steps you can take right now in the quietness of your delivery room:

1. Bow your heart before God, recognizing that you have lived your life in your own way without acknowledging His presence. Ask for His forgiveness with a sincere heart.

2. Repent of (turn away from) any specific sins that have created a barrier between you and your Creator.

3. Receive God's forgiveness and resolve to forgive others who may have hurt you or done wrong to you.

4. Accept Jesus Christ as your only Savior and Lord. Freely receive His gift of salvation.

5. Honor your Lord by obeying Him and living like a worthy daughter of God.

Sometimes it is helpful to seal such an occasion with a prayer to your heavenly Father. You can say a prayer like this:

I come to You, heavenly Father, recognizing that I am a sinner. I repent of all the wrong things I have said and done in my life. I have made a mess of things. I am genuinely sorry, and I ask for Your forgiveness. Thank You, Lord Jesus, for dying on the cross for me. I understand that You paid a high price for my redemption, and I humbly receive You today as my personal Savior and Lord. Thank You for Your forgiveness, salvation and eternal life. I invite You to come and live in my heart. Holy Spirit of God, breathe Your LIFE into my life. Teach me and guide me in Your truth now and forever. Amen.

Rejoice, woman! Today you have chosen to live eternally with your loving heavenly Father, who now waits for you with His arms wide open.

If you prayed the above prayer to receive Jesus Christ as your personal Savior, please contact our email address: editorial@christianpublications.com. We will send you the name of a local pastor who can answer any questions you may have and connect you with a local group of believers.

GLOSSARY

Abstinence
Voluntary decision to wait until marriage to have sexual activity.

Adipose tissue
Specialized connective tissue that functions as the major storage site for fat in the form of triglycerides. Adipose tissue serves three functions: heat insulation, mechanical cushion and, most importantly, a source of energy.

Albumin
Mandatory test during pregnancy that detects protein in urine. This test detects preeclampsia (pregnancy hypertensive disease).

Alkaline
Chemical compound that neutralizes acidity.

Amniotic fluid
Colorless liquid of characteristic smell that is produced, contained and renewed periodically within the amniotic sac. It protects the baby, dampening external impacts and noise. It keeps the fetus floating and promotes his harmonic anatomic development. It also helps to test some physiological functions, such as urinary system, respiratory system, digestive tract, olfaction, hearing and equilibrium systems. The amniotic fluid also facilitates the birth process and is a prenatal source of genetic information.

Amniotic sac
Membrane-like sac containing the fetus and the amniotic fluid.

Anesthesia
Medical intervention to alleviate pain for a period of time. A chemical compound is injected to temporarily inactivate the nerve ends in charge of sensations and movement. Anesthesia can be local, regional or general.

GLOSSARY

Antibodies	Protein complex produced by the immune system to fight infectious diseases.
Birth ball	A comfort tool to help women get into positions that help labor progress.
Birth canal	The passageway that the baby travels through during birth. It is made up of the cervix, vagina and vulva.
Birth philosophy	Sense of transcendence and value given to the protagonists of childbirth: mother, baby and family.
Blastocyst	Term for the developing baby when it reaches the uterus at roughly the fifth day. The blastocyst implants into the uterine wall on about day six. At this point in the mother's menstrual cycle, the endometrium (lining of the uterus) has grown and is ready to support a fetus. The blastocyst adheres tightly to the endometrium where it receives nourishment via the mother's bloodstream.
Blood pressure	The pressure of the blood within the arteries. It is produced primarily by the contraction of the heart muscle.
Blood type	Human blood can be classified in several blood types, according to the presence or absence of different antigens, such as A, B, AB or O.
Blowing	Action of forcing air through the mouth; useful during labor as a breathing technique and strategy to prevent spontaneous pushing.

Bone marrow	Spongy and highly vascular tissue inside the long bones. Red blood cells, white blood cells and platelets are formed here.
Braxton Hicks	Irregular, low-intensity uterine contractions that prepare the uterus for labor. They are more frequent during the last month.
Breakage of the water	When the amniotic sac ruptures naturally as labor begins. Medical intervention may also puncture the sac to speed up labor.
Breathing patterns	Respiratory patterns altering rhythm and depth of breathing in order to deflect attention away from pain and ensure proper oxygenation.
Bronchial tubes	Air passage tubes that go into the lungs and keep branching off into smaller and smaller tubes ending at the alveoli (sacs).
Carbohydrates	Natural substances such as sugar, starch and fiber. Carbohydrates are an important part of a healthy diet because they provide fuel for the body. Many foods rich in whole-grain carbohydrates are good sources of essential vitamins and minerals.
Cervical mucous	The secretion of the glands of the cervix. The consistency of the secretion changes with the phases of the menstrual cycle.
Cervix	Lower part of the uterus which joins with the upper part of the vagina. Normally sealed by the mucous plug.

GLOSSARY

Cesarean section

A surgical procedure in which a baby is delivered through an incision in the abdomen and uterus. Used when a woman can't give birth vaginally or if the baby is in distress.

Chemical inhibition

Chemical substances (histamine, prostagladins or similar chemical messengers) excreted by the body in response to pain and/or inflammation.

Chorionic sac

The human embryo floats inside two sacs for protection and support during its development. The outer one is the chorion or chorionic sac.

Chromosome

A visible carrier of genetic information. The three billion base pairs in the human genome are organized into twenty-four distinct, physically separate microscopic units called chromosomes. All genes are arranged linearly along the chromosomes. The nucleus of most human cells contains two sets of chromosomes, one set given by each parent. Each set has twenty-three single chromosomes—twenty-two autosomes and an X or Y sex chromosome. (A normal female will have a pair of X chromosomes; a male will have an X and Y pair.)

Cilia

The fine hairlike projections from certain cells that sweep in unison and help to sweep away fluids and particles. Some single-celled organisms use the rhythmical motion of cilia for movement.

Clavicle

The anterior portion of the shoulder girdle.

It is a long bone, curved somewhat like the italic letter *f*, and placed nearly horizontally at the upper and anterior part of the thorax, immediately above the first rib.

Colostrum

The first milk the mother's breasts produce in the early days of breast-feeding. This special milk is low in fat and high in carbohydrates, protein and antibodies to help keep the baby healthy. It is extremely easy to digest and is therefore the perfect first food for the baby.

Contraction

During labor, the strong, rhythmic tightening of the uterus. Pre-labor contractions are usually irregular and don't increase in intensity or duration.

Cycle of pain

Recurring cycle in which fear generates muscle tension and pain. In response, pain increases fear, causing more tension and pain.

Dairy products

Foods derived from milk, such as cheese, butter, ice cream and yogurt. Dairy products are a good source of carbohydrates, fats, proteins, vitamins A, B and D and calcium.

Diaphragm

Muscular structure separating chest and abdominal cavities.

Dilation

Opening of the cervix during labor.

Doppler

Doppler amplifiers are used to detect heartbeat at early stages. This instrument bounces harmless sound waves off the fetal heart. The way the sound comes back is affected by

GLOSSARY

motion, so a beating heart creates a change in the sound that can be picked up by the receiver in the Doppler.

Doula
A person trained to help a woman during labor and after the birth of the baby.

EDD (Estimated Delivery Date)
Estimated date for birth.

Edema
Swelling of limbs (mainly legs and feet) and soft tissues due to liquid retention.

Egg
A reproductive cell produced by the ovary; also called an ovum. Like its male counterpart (sperm cell), the egg has only one-half of the chromosomes of a normal cell. The two are dependent on each other to survive. The fertilized egg or primordial cell of the baby restores the chromosomes needed for reproduction, but unlike a standard cell, which reproduces only one copy of itself, the fertilized egg is able to form billions of new cells that will constitute a unique and unrepeatable human being.

Embryo
Term used for the developing baby between the second and sixth weeks of pregnancy.

Embryonic disc
A plate-like mass of cells in the blastocyst from which the embryo begins to develop in the fertilized ovum. Also called blast disk or germinal disk.

Endocrine glands
The endocrine system is made up of the endocrine glands that secrete hormones. There

are eight major endocrine glands scattered throughout the body.

Endometrium

The blood-rich mucous membrane lining the uterus (which is usually shed as your period). The embryo implants into this lining and takes early nourishment from it.

Endorphin

Powerful analgesic, chemically similar to morphine, originated in the brain after intense pain. High levels of endorphins are found in women who give birth in natural form.

Episiotomy

Medical intervention to widen the vaginal opening for delivery. This is the name of an incision made to the perineum during childbirth.

Expulsive phase

The second phase of labor, in which the baby descends from the pelvic bones to the exterior, crossing the birth canal and the perineum. Uterine contractions cause an intense and involuntary desire to push in order to speed the birthing process.

Fallopian tubes

The two narrow tubes that connect the uterus to the respective ovary. They carry the egg (fertilized or not) from the ovary to the uterus. The inner duct is as narrow as two hairs, which makes it very susceptible to obstruction due to pelvic inflammation, leading to infertility.

Fertilization

Union of a sperm and egg.

Fetus

The developing baby within the womb from the seventh week to the end of pregnancy.

GLOSSARY

First labor phase
The first phase of labor, also known as the active phase. The baby begins his descent into the pelvis, slowly dilating the cervix. It starts with a long series of irregular and ineffective contractions (pre-labor) and ends with a short phase of intense and frequent contractions (transition).

Follicle
A fluid-filled sac in the ovary that contains an egg that is released at ovulation. Each month an egg develops inside the ovary in a fluid-filled pocket called a follicle. This follicle grows to about one inch in size when it is ready to ovulate.

Food Guide Pyramid
Illustration developed by the USDA that serves as a general guide for a healthy diet. It represents six groups of foods in terms of the recommended daily intake (RDI).

Forceps
Obstetric instrument, in the shape of pincers, placed around the head of the baby to help guide his passage through the birth canal.

Formula
Cow milk formulated to resemble human milk composition in terms of fat, proteins and minerals. Formula milk cannot supply the hundreds of nutrients and compounds that human milk has.

Gate Control Theory
The process of massaging or rubbing to "close the gate" that pain impulses have to pass through. Pain impulses run toward the spinal cord and then up the cord and into the brain.

It's only when they reach the brain that these impulses are perceived as pain. When you rub, it sends other impulses along the same nerves. When all these impulses try to reach the brain through nerves, the nerves get clogged. The result? Most of them won't reach the brain. And if the pain signals do not reach the brain, you won't feel pain.

Genetic material   DNA that is passed from parents to children.

HCG   The blastocyst secretes a hormone called human chorionic gonadotropin (HCG) that stimulates the mother's ovary to continue producing progesterone, which acts to maintain the lining of the uterus so that the embryo will continue to be nourished.

Hiccups   Involuntary and periodic contractions of the diaphragm.

Hormones   A chemical secretion, such as estrogen or progesterone, that the body produces to stimulate or slow down various body functions. The levels of some hormones increase tenfold during pregnancy.

Humectant   Substance that promotes the conservation of humidity. Humectant creams contain substances of this kind (glycerin, sorbitol, etc.).

Hyoid bone   A single small U-shaped bone that does not connect with any other bone. It is located at the front of the throat and beneath the mandible but above the larynx.

GLOSSARY

Immune system
The network of cells, organs and tissues that defend the body against infection and disease.

Implantation
Approximately eight days after ovulation, if pregnant, the blastocyst (as the baby is classified at this stage) begins to secrete a hormone that enables it to burrow into the lining of the uterus. Implantation usually happens in the upper one-third of the uterus, and the placenta will then begin to form.

Inguinal rings
When a male baby is developing, the testes grow and form inside his abdominal cavity. Around the seventh month of pregnancy, the testes descend out of the abdominal cavity via a small hole in the inner layer of the wall on either side—called the inguinal rings—and into the scrotum.

Kegel exercises
Rhythmic exercises of the pelvic floor recommended for the strengthening of the perineum before, during and after labor. The Kegel exercises can be conducted by tightening and relaxing the muscles used to control the flow of urine.

Labor
Set of symptoms and signs during the process of childbirth. It starts with irregular contractions and culminates with the expulsion of the placenta and the birth of the baby.

Labor and delivery phases
First (Active) phase: Descent of the baby to the pelvis (encasing), slowly dilating the

cervix. It starts with a long series of irregular and ineffective contractions (pre-labor) and ends with a short phase of intense and frequent contractions (transition).

Second (Expulsive) phase: The baby descends from the pelvic bones to the exterior, crossing the birth canal and the perineum. Uterine contractions cause an intense and involuntary desire to push in order to speed the birthing process.

Third phase (Birth): Spontaneous expulsion of the amniotic sac and placenta. Early breast-feeding accelerates this phase and triggers the "coming down of milk" reflex.

Lactation The production of milk by the mammary glands for the purpose of nursing. Breast-feeding gives a baby overwhelming health and emotional benefits.

Lamaze Last name of a French obstetrician/gynecologist who studied and developed physiological strategies to face the pain of labor and delivery. After nearly fifty years, this is an international organization with a mission to promote, support and protect natural birth through education and advocacy.

Lanugo Smooth, temporary hair covering shoulders, back, forehead and cheeks of the fetus. It disappears by the end of pregnancy. Premature babies can be distinguished by the presence of lanugo.

GLOSSARY

Laxative	Substance capable of accelerating the passing of foods along the intestines.
Mandible	The bone of the lower jaw.
Meconium	First bowel movement of the baby. It is a greenish substance that accumulates inside the fetus's intestines and is evacuated soon after birth. The presence of a yellow-greenish coloration in the amniotic fluid is a sign of fetal suffering due to lack of oxygen. Colostrum (the first maternal milk) facilitates evacuation of meconium and prevents cramps for the baby.
Medical interventions	Invasive procedures substituting or supporting some part of labor and delivery in order to save the mother's or baby's life.
Menstruation	The periodic discharge of blood, tissue, fluid and mucous from the reproductive organs of sexually mature females. The flow usually lasts from three to six days each month and is caused by a sudden reduction in the hormones estrogen and progesterone.
Midwife	A woman skilled in aiding the delivery of babies.
Miscarriage	The involuntary loss of a pregnancy before twenty weeks, estimated to end fifteen to twenty percent of all pregnancies. More than eighty percent of miscarriages occur in the first twelve weeks of pregnancy, many before a woman even knows she's pregnant.
Morning sickness	Nausea and vomiting that affects fifty to eighty percent of pregnant women.

Morula	When cell division has generated about sixteen cells, the zygote becomes a morula (mulberry shaped). The morula is a solid ball; after the sixty-four-cell phase, it develops into a hollow ball, the blastocyst.
Mucous plug	Semi-solid plug sealing the cervix against any infection. As the cervix begins to open and thin for labor, the mucous plug can dislodge. It may be tinged with blood.
Nipple confusion	The problem that arises when a breast-fed baby is given an artificial (rubber or silicon) nipple and must try to learn to nurse from both his mother's breast and the bottle nipple. While seemingly similar, these two feeding methods require completely different mouth and tongue motions and swallowing skills.
Nurse cells	Nourishing cells responsible for providing nourishment to the spermatids (immature sperm).
Nutrients	Elemental nutritive substances found in foods. The nutrients known to be essential for human beings are proteins, carbohydrates, fats and oils, minerals, vitamins and water.
Occipital bone	The bone that forms the rear and the rear bottom of the skull.
Ossification	Conversion of fibrous tissue or cartilage into bone.
Ovaries	The female reproductive organs that release

GLOSSARY

eggs into the fallopian tubes where, if sperm is present, they may be fertilized.

Oxytocin

Hormone secreted by the brain's pituitary gland after receiving the signal of completed fetal maturity. Its main function is to start uterine contractions and mother-child bonding. Pitocin is the commercial version of this hormone.

Pelvic floor muscles

A series of muscles that form a sling across the opening of the pelvis. These muscles, together with their surrounding tissue, are responsible for keeping all of the pelvic organs (bladder, uterus and rectum) in place and functioning correctly.

Pericardium

A double-layer sac surrounding the heart and part of the great vessels. Tubular extensions of the pericardium surround the ascending aorta, pulmonary artery, pulmonary veins and vena cavae.

Perineum

Group of muscles forming the pelvic floor and supporting the pelvic organs. The perineum is a sort of hammock that surrounds the vagina, rectum and urethra and facilitates their function. It has great importance for the expulsive phase of labor.

Placenta

Fetal organ that joins mother and fetus through the umbilical cord. It is a disc-shaped organ weighing around one pound by the end of pregnancy. The placenta performs many functions but mainly allows the supply of oxygen and nutrients to flow from the mother to the baby without blending each other's blood. The placenta also filters almost all harmful materials coming from the mother or from the baby's waste. It also produces hormones, among many other functions.

Portion(s)
Unit used to define the typical consumption amount of a certain food group. For instance, in the case of liquids, "portion" is equivalent to an eight-fluid-ounce glass; for meat, "portion" represents one hundred grams. A "portion" of fruit typically represents one unit of the corresponding fruit, and so on. Pre-packaged foods by law must provide certain nutritional information, including the definition of "portion." This term is closely associated with the concept of the Food Guide Pyramid.

Posterior presentation
Postion in which the fetus is facing the mother's belly instead of her back. Mothers of babies in the posterior position are more likely to have long and painful labors as the baby usually has to turn all the way around in order to be born. Cephalic presentation is normal and implies the baby's head is opening the birth canal. When the baby's buttocks or legs come first, it is called pelvic or breech presentation. This type of presentation is rare and takes place in about five percent of childbirths.

Preeclampsia
Formerly known as toxemia, preeclampsia is a condition characterized by high blood pressure and protein in the urine after the twentieth

week of pregnancy. A serious condition if left untreated, preeclampsia can lead to complications or death in the mother or baby.

Prenatal vitamins A supplement taken daily to ensure a pregnant woman is getting the right amount of nutrients during pregnancy. These contain more of certain nutrients such as folic acid and iron.

Progesterone Maternity hormone that is present after ovulation. It increases when conception occurs.

Prostatic fluid Liquid secreted by the prostate gland and one of the liquid components of semen. Can induce uterine contractions.

Pushing Action evacuating the contents of a hollow organ to the exterior of the body through an orifice called the sphincter.

Rebozo Commonly used as a baby sling, rebozos have multi-purpose functions as pregnancy and labor tools. Mexican women have used them for years to help support a very pregnant and pendulous belly, as a massage tool for lower back pain, and to help with changing the position of a posterior-positioned or even a breech baby. During labor a rebozo is more commonly used during the second stage, helping the mother push effectively in a "tug-of-war" position.

Relaxation Action of conscientiously relieving stress. Voluntary relaxation techniques help to reduce stress, pain and fear during labor.

Relaxin A hormone that allows pelvic expansion

to accommodate the enlarging uterus. As pregnancy progresses, it increases tenfold, reaching its peak at the fourteenth week.

Rh negative

When a woman has a negative Rh factor and her husband has a positive Rh factor, they can produce a child who is Rh positive. While the mother's and baby's blood systems are separate, there are times when the blood from the baby can enter into the mother's system. This can cause the mother to create antibodies against the Rh factor, thus treating an Rh positive baby like an intruder in her body. Many practitioners recommend giving the mother an injection of Rh-immune globulin (also known as RhIg and RhoGAM) at twenty-eight weeks' gestation to prevent the few cases of sensitization that occur at the end of pregnancy. Each dose of RhIg lasts about twelve weeks. The mother will also be given RhIg within seventy-two hours of birth if the child is Rh positive. A similar maternal antibody-induced hemolytic anemia can also result when the mother's blood type is Type O and the baby's is Type A or B; in general, these anemias are not as severe and rarely cause jaundice severe enough to require exchange transfusion.

Seminal fluid

Semen is made up of seminal fluid and sperm. The fluid comes from the prostate, seminal vesicle and other sex glands. The sperm are manufactured in the testicles. The seminal

GLOSSARY

fluid helps transport the sperm during orgasm. Seminal fluid contains sugar as an energy source for sperm.

Sexual inheritance Exclusive paternal heritage that determines the sexual identity of the new human being. Sperm cells with sexual chromosome "X" will beget girls, while sexual chromosomes "Y" engender males.

Sexuality The expression of sexual feelings due to genetic predisposition.

Somites From the Greek word meaning "little bodies." These are condensations composed of mesoderm, which appear on either side of the neural groove of the embryo, resembling bumps. These will eventually develop into the bones, muscles and dermis of and surrounding the axial skeleton.

Sperm cell The male sexual cell. The mature sperm cell is 0.05 millimeter long. It consists of a head, body and tail. The head is covered by the cap and contains a nucleus of dense genetic material from the twenty-three chromosomes. Also called male gamete and spermatozoan.

Striae Marks caused by excessive stretching of the skin.

Surfactant Soapy material found in the alveoli (final branching of the respiratory ducts) of adults and mature infants. Without surfactant the lungs would collapse after exhaling air. Production of surfactant takes place during weeks thirty-four to thirty-eight of pregnancy. Premature babies do not have enough surfactant in their lungs, causing severe respiratory problems.

Testicles

The testicles (also called testes or gonads) are the male sex glands. They produce and store sperm, and they are also the body's main source of male hormones (testosterone).

Thymus

Gland located in the base of the neck behind the sternum. It plays an important role to build up the immune system.

Transition

Transition is the most difficult phase of labor for most women. Physically, the mother is experiencing contractions two to three minutes apart, lasting sixty to ninety seconds, and they are very strong in intensity. During transition, labor support is crucial for the mother's physical and emotional well-being.

Ultrasound

Non-invasive technique widely used in obstetrics to visualize the fetal body through the use of sound waves. Ultrasound uses sound waves beyond the range of the human ear to create images of the organs inside the body. When the waves bounce against the body's internal structures, they are collected and analyzed by the machine, which constructs an image based on such information.

Umbilical cord

Long tube-like structure that transports oxygen and nutrients between the baby and the placenta.

GLOSSARY

Underwater birth Giving birth to a baby underwater. This method is a "natural alternative" to routine hospital deliveries. Some people think it offers pain relief for some mothers.

Uterine height Measurement beginning at the bottom of the uterus toward the edge of the pubic bone. It serves to determine the age and the development of the pregnancy.

Uterus Muscular pelvic organ of the female reproductive system in which the fetus develops. The lining of the uterus (endometrium) provides nutrients for the developing baby. It possesses great elasticity, according to the size of the baby. The uterus contracts in response to the oxytocin hormone, pushing the baby to the bottom of the cervix, toward the birth canal, given a ten-centimeter dilation. It takes approximately five weeks after birth for it to return to its original size and position. It is also called the womb.

Vagina The lower part of the female reproductive tract.

Vaginal canal The muscular canal extending from the uterus to the exterior of the body. Also called the birth canal.

Varicose veins Dilation of the veins, usually on the legs, due to the rupture of the small valves preventing backflow of blood inside veins. Many pregnant women experience additional vein dilation on legs, perineum or hemorrhoids due to poor posture, crossing legs (for instance) and lack of exercise. This condition is more frequent during pregnancy due to the incremental pressure exerted by the growing uterus on the pelvis's major veins. Severity of varicose veins varies from person to person and can be inherited.

Vernix Oily substance that covers and protects the baby's skin while in the uterus. Some babies are born with abundant vernix on their skin, which will become transparent when it comes in contact with air. It has moisturizing and antiseptic properties that protect the baby's delicate skin during birth. It should not be removed completely but simply rinsed off with lukewarm water.

Womb Another term for the uterus.

Yellow body Once a follicle has been impregnated, it breaks open to expose the egg. The follicle quickly transforms into the yellow body (also called *corpus luteum*) and begins to secrete progesterone and estrogen, which is used to alert the uterus wall and stimulate it to produce a mucous lining capable of accepting a fertilized egg.

Yolk sac A membrane outside the embryo but connected by a tube through the umbilical opening to the embryo. The yolk sac serves as an early site for the formation of blood.

Zygote Name given to the fertilized egg during the first days following conception.

My Pregnancy Journal

My Pregnancy Journal

My Pregnancy Journal

My Pregnancy Journal

ABOUT THE AUTHOR

Born in Colombia, Dr. Astrid Rivera is a medical surgeon with post-graduate degrees in community and occupational health from Israel, healthcare administration from Colombia and perinatal education from Mexico.

Dr. Rivera is also a certified health educator specializing in teenage pregnancy and nursing mothers. Her "Encounter with Life" bio-ethic seminars have been presented in schools, universities and youth groups in Mexico, the United States, Colombia and Spain. These value-based seminars bring awareness on the spiritual meaning of biological moments and life decisions. As an abstinence/perinatal educator, counselor and adviser at pregnancy crisis centers, Astrid also contributes to research projects for Kennesaw State University (KSU).

Dr. Rivera and her husband are state Latino directors of The University of the Family, an international non-profit organization operating in eighty-eight countries. She is also founder and director of ABBA, School of Mothers.

Her most important project, however, is being a wife and mother of three young daughters. The family currently resides in Kennesaw, Georgia.